JE915.493 Wel
Lee, Vanessa.

Welcome to Sri Lanka

WITHDRAWN

150 N. Whipple Street
Fort Wayne IN 46714

WELCOME TO MY COUNTRY

Welcome to
SRI LANKA

Gareth Stevens Publishing
A WORLD ALMANAC EDUCATION GROUP COMPANY

SALINE DISTRICT LIBRARY
555 N. Maple Road
Saline, MI 48176

Written by
VANESSA LEE/KRISHNAN GURUSWAMY

Edited by
MELVIN NEO

Edited in USA by
JOANN EARLY MACKEN

Designed by
GEOSLYN LIM

Picture research by
SUSAN JANE MANUEL

First published in North America in 2003 by
Gareth Stevens Publishing
A World Almanac Education Group Company
330 West Olive Street, Suite 100
Milwaukee, Wisconsin 53212 USA

Please visit our web site at:
www.garethstevens.com
For a free color catalog describing
Gareth Stevens Publishing's list of high-quality
books and multimedia programs,
call 1-800-542-2595 (USA) or
1-800-387-3178 (Canada).
Gareth Stevens Publishing's fax: (414) 332-3567.

All rights reserved. No parts of this book may be reproduced or
utilized in any form or by any means electronic or mechanical,
including photocopying, recording, or by an information storage and
retrieval system, without permission from the copyright owner.

© **TIMES MEDIA PRIVATE LIMITED 2003**
Originated and designed by
Times Editions
An imprint of Times Media Private Limited
A member of the Times Publishing Group
Times Centre, 1 New Industrial Road
Singapore 536196
http://www.timesone.com.sg/te

Library of Congress Cataloging-in-Publication Data
Lee, Vanessa.
Welcome to Sri Lanka / Vanessa Lee and Krishnan Guruswamy.
p. cm. — (Welcome to my country)
Contents: Welcome to Sri Lanka! — The land — History —
Government and the economy — People and lifestyle —
Language — Arts — Leisure — Food.
Includes bibliographical references and index.
ISBN 0-8368-2554-3 (lib. bdg.)
1. Sri Lanka—Juvenile literature. [1. Sri Lanka.]
I. Guruswamy, Krishnan. II. Title. III. Series.
DS489.L34   2003
954.93—dc21   2003050381

Printed in Singapore

1 2 3 4 5 6 7 8 9 07 06 05 04 03

PICTURE CREDITS
Art Directors & TRIP Photo Library: 9
   (bottom), 10, 11, 14, 17, 27 (bottom),
   30, 31, 35, 37, 39 (bottom), 43
Camera Press: 9 (top), 15 (bottom), 24
CPA Media: cover, 3 (top), 5, 7, 8, 19, 20
   (bottom), 28, 40
Alain Evrard: 45
Focus Team — Italy: 1, 3 (bottom), 26,
   27 (top), 33
GV-Press: 3 (center), 22
HBL Network Photo Agency: 6, 39 (top)
The Hutchison Library: 4, 25, 29, 34
   (bottom), 38
Image Solutions: 2, 20 (top), 32
Earl Kowall: 21, 23, 34 (top)
North Wind Picture Archives: 12
Topham Picturepoint: 13, 15 (top and center),
   16, 18 (both), 36, 41

Digital Scanning by Superskill Graphics Pte Ltd

Contents

Words that appear in the glossary are printed in **boldface** type the first time they occur in the text.

Welcome to Sri Lanka!

The Dutch called this country Ceylan, while the British knew it as Ceylon. The Sinhalese called it Lanka, and to the Tamils, it was Ilankai. In 1972, the prefix *sri,* meaning "favorable" in Sinhala, was added. Let's explore Sri Lanka and learn about its history and culture.

Opposite: In Sri Lanka, shops by the roadside sell a variety of snacks.

Below: Fishermen pull in their nets. Fishing is a source of food and also a means of income for people living near the ocean.

The Flag of Sri Lanka

The green stripe in the left panel represents Sri Lanka's Muslims. The orange stripe represents the Tamils. On the right, the lion represents the Sinhalese people, and the leaves at each corner symbolize Buddhism, the country's main religion.

The Land

Sri Lanka covers an area of 25,332 square miles (65,610 square kilometers). The country is in the Indian Ocean south of India. The Maldives lie to the west, and Singapore, Malaysia, and Indonesia lie far to the east.

The teardrop-shaped island of Sri Lanka has beaches, mountains, dense forests, and arid plains. The lush hills also contain the country's tea estates.

Below: The town of Galle, located along the southern coast of Sri Lanka, is popular with both local and foreign tourists.

Lagoons and bays line the southern, southeastern, and western coasts of Sri Lanka. The northeastern coast features several deep harbors. The mountainous south-central region is surrounded by flat coastal plains. The country's highest mountain, Pidurutalagala, is 8,281 feet (2,524 meters) high. Two **plateaus** in the same area contain many tea plantations. Sri Lanka's longest river is the Mahaweli Ganga.

Above: Tea is one of the country's major exports. Tea estates are found in the hills around the town of Nuwara Eliya in central Sri Lanka.

Climate

Sri Lanka's climate is generally hot and humid. In May and June, temperatures can rise to 95° Fahrenheit (35° Celsius). Most months, lowland temperatures remain at about 90° F (32° C). The temperature in the mountains stays at about 70° F (21° C). In most parts of the country, the average annual rainfall is 99 inches (251cm). A dry, rolling plain stretches from the mountains to the northern tip of the island.

Above: Sri Lanka's humid climate is suitable for flowers such as water hyacinths and orchids to grow.

Plants and Animals

Ferns, water hyacinths, orchids, and other beautiful plants thrive in Sri Lanka. Mahogany and other timber trees grow in wet areas. Ebony and satinwood trees grow in drier places. Elephants, monkeys, porcupines, sloth bears, jackals, and flying foxes live in the country. Many animals live in wildlife **sanctuaries**. More than sixty kinds of fish live in the inland lakes, and about one thousand species live around the island. Sri Lanka has more than four hundred species of birds.

Above: There are between 2,500 and 3,000 elephants in Sri Lanka. A special elephant **orphanage** houses animals whose homes have been destroyed.

Below: Monkeys sometimes live in the remains of ruined buildings in Sri Lanka.

History

The earliest people to settle in Sri Lanka were the Wanniyala-Aettos or *Veddahs* (VED-duhs). Most people believe that the Sinhalese from northern India came in the fifth or sixth century B.C. The Tamils from southern India invaded Sri Lanka several times until the twelfth century. They eventually established a kingdom in the northern part of the country.

Below: Because Sri Lanka has a very long and rich history, ruins of ancient palaces such as this one in Polonnaruwa are a common sight.

In the next two centuries, the Sinhalese held power. Other forces also attacked the island before the Europeans arrived.

Above: Kandy was one of the few areas to escape capture by the Portuguese in the sixteenth century. The rulers of Kandy entered into an agreement with the Dutch to get rid of the Portuguese in Sri Lanka.

Colonial Period

Between 1505 and 1945, Sri Lanka was ruled by the Portuguese, the Dutch, and the British. By 1518, the Portuguese had built a fort in Sri Lanka and were given trading rights. Through various means, the Portuguese controlled all of Sri Lanka, except for Kandy, by 1619.

Left:
Workers on a plantation in Sri Lanka sort dried tea leaves.

Dutch Rule

With the help of the Dutch, the Sri Lankans fought the Portuguese for about twenty years. In 1658, the Dutch gained control of most of Sri Lanka, except Kandy. The Dutch concentrated on trade and left the locals alone.

British Rule

In 1796, British forces defeated the Dutch. By 1815, the British gained control of the whole country. They set up coffee, tea, and coconut plantations and built railroads to transport crops. They taught English in the schools.

Sri Lanka fought to gain independence and was given limited control over its national affairs in 1931.

Independence

The British granted Sri Lanka its independence in 1947. A new government was formed, and its first prime minister was Don Stephen Senanayake. An ancient Sinhalese flag was adopted as the new national flag.

Below: Solomon West Ridgeway Dias Bandaranaike (*second from right*) was Sri Lanka's prime minister from 1956 to 1959. He passed many laws that favored the country's Sinhalese people, leading to civil war with the Tamil population many years later.

Civil War

Trouble started in 1960 when Prime Minister Sirimavo Bandaranaike made Sinhala the country's official language. When she continued to favor the Sinhalese, the Tamils formed rebel groups. By 1983, the Liberation Tigers of Tamil Eelam (LTTE) had become the strongest group. LTTE actions caused a riot, which led to a civil war. The current prime minister promised to hold peace talks with the LTTE.

Below: Sri Lankan government forces and Tamil rebel groups have been fighting each other in a civil war since 1983. Five rounds of peace talks have been held. The latest meeting took place in Berlin in February 2003.

Solomon West Ridgeway Dias Bandaranaike (1899–1959)

Sri Lanka's first prime minister promoted the arts and defended the rights of the poor. His decisions in favor of the Sinhalese angered the Tamil minority. He was **assassinated** in 1959 by a Sinhalese monk.

S. W. R. D. Bandaranaike

Sirimavo Ratwatte Dias Bandaranaike (1916–2000)

After her husband was assassinated in 1960, Bandaranaike became prime minister. Her policies still favored the Sinhalese, which angered the Tamils. She was reelected in 1994.

Sirimavo Ratwatte Dias Bandaranaike

Velupillai Prabhakaran (1954–)

Prabhakaran is the leader of the Tamil Tigers. This **guerilla** group wants to create an independent Tamil homeland called "Eelam," which means "precious land" in Tamil. The group has been blamed for several bombings.

Velupillai Prabhakaran

Government and the Economy

Sri Lanka is a democratic nation with a president and a national government elected by the people. The **parliament** has only one house with 225 seats. Its members serve for six years. Each of Sri Lanka's nine **provinces** has a local government, called a provincial council, elected by the people. The president chooses a governor to head the council.

Below: The former parliament building in the capital city of Colombo houses offices for the president's staff. Colombo is the legislative and business center of Sri Lanka.

Left:
William Gopallawa
(1897–1981) was
Sri Lanka's first
president. The
country's president
is both the chief of
state and the head
of government.

The Legal System

Sri Lanka's legal system has several
levels of courts. Judges serve on the
Supreme Court, the Court of Appeal,
the High Court, and other lower courts.

Political Parties

There are more than twenty political
parties in Sri Lanka. In the 2001
parliamentary elections, the United
National Party won the majority vote,
with 45 percent. Another **prominent**
political party is the People's Alliance,
which is made up of several groups.

Left: In the 1970s, agriculture formed the bulk of exports in Sri Lanka. The government has **diversified** into other industries, and today, agriculture only accounts for 20 percent of exports.

The Economy

From the time that Sri Lanka became independent in 1948 until 1977, the government ran the schools, bus and train services, hospitals, and other businesses. In 1977, private companies began to set up operations there. The economy is weak, and nearly 9 percent of the people are unemployed. In addition, 22 percent of the people live in poverty. The civil war in Sri Lanka has caused tourism to decline.

Above: Sri Lanka is the nation with the largest number of gemstones in one place. More than fifty types of gems, including diamonds, sapphires, and rubies, are found on the island.

The main exports of Sri Lanka are clothing, tea, gems, and spices. Its main industries include agriculture, clothing, cement, fabrics, petroleum refining, tobacco, and services. Government jobs that ensure employment and **pension** benefits are in great demand. Many people work in factories or as domestic helpers overseas, where they can earn more money. Those who work in other countries often send money home.

Below: Most major towns and cities in Sri Lanka are linked by train. The train network in the country measures 909 miles (1,463 km) long.

People and Lifestyle

The earliest settlers of Sri Lanka were the Veddahs. About 2,500 Veddahs still live in the southeastern forests of the country. The four main **ethnic** groups are the Sinhalese (74 percent), the Tamils (18 percent), the Moors or Muslims (7 percent), and the **Burghers** (less than 1 percent).

Above and below: The sari (*above*) is the traditional dress of Sri Lanka. On regular days, however, women wear Western-style clothing.

The Sinhalese came to Sri Lanka around the fifth century B.C. from northern India. From around the third century A.D., the Tamils from southern

India started invading the country. They built a kingdom in northern Sri Lanka. Moors are thought to be the descendants of Arab and Muslim Indian traders. The Burghers are a group of people who are descended from the Dutch and Portuguese rulers.

In addition, Sri Lanka is home to a small number of people of other ethnic groups, such as the Chinese, the Malays, and people from other European countries.

Above: Families in Sri Lanka are very close, and it is common for several generations of a family to live together, especially in rural areas.

Family Life

Most Sri Lankans used to live in homes with many members of their families. Because Western ideas have become more common and cities have gotten larger, however, today's families are smaller. Divorce is rare in Sri Lanka. Parents often decide what their children should study and what careers they should pursue. Children respect their elders, and most young adults obey their parents' wishes.

Above:
Sri Lankan children are expected to obey their parents, even when they become adults.

Boys and girls rarely go out on dates or choose their own partners. Holding hands in public is frowned upon. Most marriages in Sri Lanka are arranged by the parents. Parents might advertise in a newspaper for a husband or wife for their child. Before many marriages, an **astrologer** compares the two people's **horoscopes**. The bride's family often pays a dowry, such as cash or land, to the groom's family.

Below: Marriages in Sri Lanka are arranged by family members, and most couples only meet briefly before the wedding ceremony.

Education

All children between the ages of five and fourteen must attend school. Most children spend five years in elementary school, two years in high school, and two years in pre-university classes. The students study English and either Tamil or Sinhalese. They also take classes in subjects such as math, life sciences, and social studies. Many students have private tutoring classes after school.

Below: Children attend classes that are taught by a Buddhist monk. As they grow older, children may attend private classes in math and science and try to get higher grades so they can qualify to enter a top university.

Universities in Sri Lanka offer degrees in many subjects. The most popular programs are medicine, law, engineering, and computer science. All forms of education in Sri Lanka are free. Students who do not attend a university may try to learn a trade, such as carpentry. Some wealthy families send their children to another country, such as India, Canada, England, the United States, or Australia, for their higher education.

Above: Over 90 percent of all Sri Lankans can read and write. Not all women attend school, however, so only about 83 percent of the women can read and write.

Above: Sri Lankan boys attend a class on Buddhism in a Buddhist temple.

Religion

The four main religions practiced in Sri Lanka are Buddhism, Hinduism, Christianity, and Islam. Children attend religious classes while in school, and each school day begins with a prayer. Many schools include prayers of the four main religions.

Buddhism

About 70 percent of all Sri Lankans are Buddhists. Buddhism focuses on love, compassion, and gentleness.

Buddhism was founded in the sixth century B.C. by an Indian prince, who became known as the Buddha.

Above: Muslim boys and men must wear a special headdress called a *ketayap* (kur-TAH-yahp) when attending religious events.

Other Religions

Hinduism was brought to Sri Lanka from Southern India by the Tamils. About 15 percent of Sri Lankans practice Hinduism. The Portuguese **colonizers** brought Christianity to the country. About 8 percent of Sri Lankans are Christians. Arab and Indian traders brought Islam to Sri Lanka. About 7 percent of the people are Muslims, or followers of Islam.

Left: Roman Catholicism was introduced to Sri Lanka in the sixteenth century by the Portuguese. Some Catholic churches re-create scenes from the Bible during Easter and Christmas.

Language

Sri Lanka has two national languages, Sinhala, or Sinhalese, and Tamil. Three-fourths of the people speak Sinhala. Three to four million people speak Tamil. Few Sri Lankans speak English, although many understand it. Sri Lanka has its own special English phrases, such as "short eats" for snack. The English word "cash" comes from a Tamil word for money.

Below:
These street signs are written in Sinhala, which is based on an ancient language called Sanskrit.

Literature

Ancient Sinhalese and Tamil stories were written on palm leaves. Between the tenth and thirteenth centuries, the stories told of kings and the Buddha. From the fifteenth to the nineteenth centuries, the Sinhalese wrote poetry to express their views. In later years, Sinhalese and Tamil writers wrote stories and textbooks on medicine and science. Many recent Sri Lankan authors live outside the country.

Above: Sri Lankans enjoy reading. Most Sri Lankan authors write in Sinhalese or Tamil.

Arts

Music

Sri Lankans enjoy listening to what they call light music—pop music and music from the movies. Some light music comes from street theater and southern Indian classical music. The British introduced Western classical music to the country. Today, theater and music groups in Sri Lanka perform operas and other types of music from all over the world.

Below: *Baila* (BY-lah) is a form of music found only in Sri Lanka. With a lively beat and throbbing drums, the music sounds a bit like Caribbean calypso. As they sing, performers can make up new lyrics, so there are many versions of baila songs.

Left: Sri Lankans enjoy watching movies. Movie tickets are cheap, and many theaters in Sri Lanka show both local and foreign films.

Movies

Early Sri Lankan movies were often local versions of foreign movies. The first movie in Sinhalese, *Broken Promise*, was made in 1947. Since then, movie directors have produced many films with local stories and even addressed social issues. Today, the leading film directors in Sri Lanka are Lester James Peiris, Vasantha Obeysekera, and H. D. Premaratne.

Dance

The Kandyan dance, popular during the Kandyan era, is the country's national dance. It features bare-chested male dancers in wide skirts and silver and ivory necklaces. Female dancers wear skirts and short blouses with silver **embroidery**. The dancers twirl and leap as drums play complex rhythms.

Handicrafts

Wooden masks and mats made of plant fiber are important handicrafts in Sri Lanka. Many people there make and use earthen pots for cooking food.

Architecture

Buddhist shrines are found in northern Sri Lanka. These brick structures are covered with a layer of white plaster and are shaped like bells or domes. *Kovils* (KOH-vills), or Hindu temples, are dedicated to Shiva, the god of destruction. They include a prayer hall and a shrine room. The country also has European-style forts and churches.

Above:
Batik printing is a traditional Sri Lankan craft that requires a lot of skill and patience.

Opposite:
A traditional dance performance in Sri Lanka. Other dances that are rarely performed are the devil dance for **exorcising** spirits and the *kolam* (KOH-lahm), a masked dance.

Leisure

Sri Lankan children often make up simple games, such as throwing rocks at a target or rolling tires down a slope.

Traditional Activities

Traditional games are played at New Year celebrations. In ***kotta pora*** (koh-TAH POH-rah), or pillow fighting, contestants sit on a pole and try to knock each other off with pillows. In rural areas, grandparents gather their grandchildren to tell folktales.

Above: Although cycling is popular in Sri Lanka, it can be dangerous because many roads are in bad condition.

Left: In batik printing, designs are drawn on cloth with melted wax, and then the patterns are dyed in bright colors.

Indoor Activities

Checkers, chess, and variations of Monopoly are popular indoor games for those living in cities. An indoor game called *olinda kaliya* (oh-LIN-dah KAH-lee-yah) is played with red seeds on a wooden board.

Outdoor Fun

Sri Lanka has many beaches, rivers, and lakes. Swimming, fishing, and taking walks in the country are all popular outdoor activities.

Above: Sri Lankans enjoy spending time at home with their family members.

Sports

Sri Lanka offers many sports, including **cricket**, cycling, and golf. Cricket is the most popular sport, especially since 1996, when the Sri Lankan cricket team won the Cricket World Cup. Children practice on tiny patches of land. Eager fans pack stadiums during the cricket season, which runs from September to April. Bicycles can be rented in most cities so cyclists can view the country at close range.

Above: The Sri Lanka cricket team competes against England in the 1996 Cricket World Cup.

The Sri Lankan Airlines Golf Classic tournament is held every year for local and foreign players. Tennis courts are available at hotels and tennis clubs.

Water Sports

Sri Lankans and tourists visit the country's beautiful beaches. Water sports such as diving and **snorkeling** attract people to spots near Galle and Colombo. In the clear water, divers can see coral reefs with amazing marine life and even explore shipwrecks.

Below: Basketball is another popular sport in Sri Lanka. Some Sri Lankans play with friends, in local leagues, and in competitions.

New Year Celebrations

The Sri Lankan New Year falls on April 14, which is the end of the harvest season. Celebrations start in the morning. At a time set by a priest and announced on television, the first fire of the year is lighted in the hearth. People wear new clothes, and families eat a meal together. To welcome the new year, children set off firecrackers. Later, families visit neighbors and relatives with fruit baskets and gifts.

Below: A Hindu priest leads a woman in a chant during a temple festival.

Other Festivals

Vesak, the main Buddhist festival, is based on the life and death of Buddha. The major Hindu festival, *Deepavali*, marks the triumph of good over evil. Hindus celebrate a harvest festival in January. For *Thaipusam*, (THIGH-poo-sum), Hindus fast and pray for one month. Muslims observe Ramadan with a month of fasting and prayer. Christians in Sri Lanka celebrate Christmas and Good Friday.

Above and below: The Perahera festival in Kandy features lively processions and fireworks. The celebrations last for ten days in July or August.

Food

Traditional breakfasts in Sri Lanka might include *hoppers* (hop-PERS), string hoppers, or *pittu* (pit-TOOH). To make hoppers, rice batter is cooked in small earthen bowls. Hoppers are sometimes eaten with eggs or vegetable stew. String hoppers are steamed rice circles eaten with spicy gravy. Pittu, made from rice flour and coconut, is steamed in bamboo tubes.

Below: Spices are important ingredients in most Sri Lankan dishes. The country also exports its spices all over the world.

Lunch and dinner in Sri Lanka are often rice with curry. Silverware is sometimes used, but traditional Sri Lankans eat with their right hands. The country grows more than one thousand types of tea, and tea is a favorite drink.

Many tropical fruits, such as pineapples and mangoes, grow in Sri Lanka. Rambutan is a red, spiny fruit the size of a walnut. Favorite desserts include egg pudding, rice flour fudge, and yogurt with palm syrup.

Above: A stall owner sells fried snacks. Vegetable or meat rolls and deep-fried lentil patties are Sri Lankan snacks.

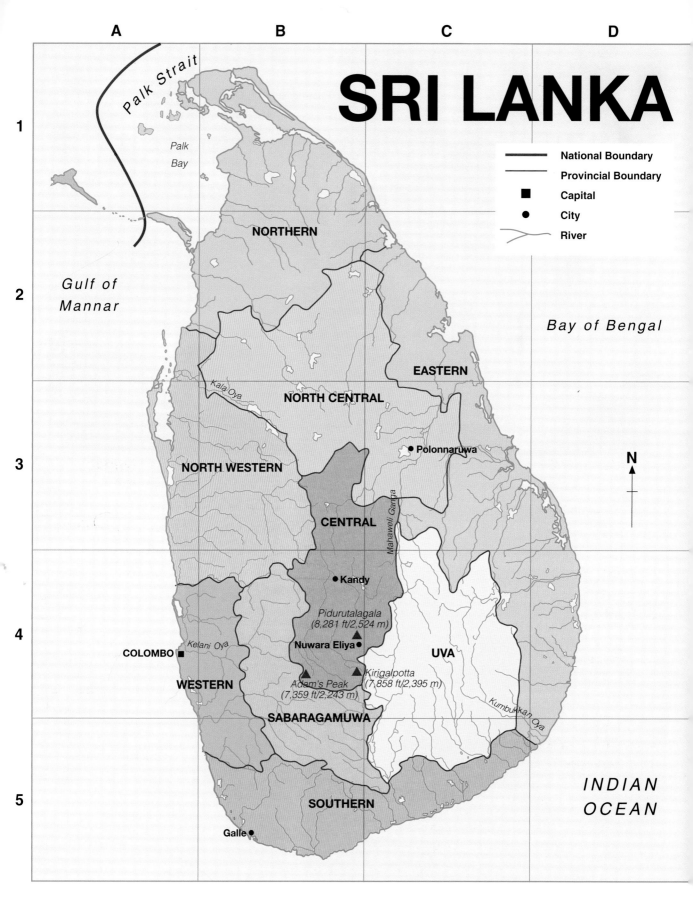

SRI LANKA

	National Boundary
	Provincial Boundary
■	Capital
●	City
~~	River

Palk Strait

Palk Bay

NORTHERN

Gulf of Mannar

Bay of Bengal

EASTERN

Kala Oya

NORTH CENTRAL

● Polonnaruwa

NORTH WESTERN

N

CENTRAL

Mahaweli Ganga

● Kandy

Pidurutalagala (8,281 ft/2,524 m) ▲

Kelani Oya

COLOMBO ■

Nuwara Eliya ●

UVA

WESTERN

▲ *Adam's Peak (7,359 ft/2,243 m)*

▲ Kirigalpotta *(7,858 ft/2,395 m)*

Kumbukkan Oya

SABARAGAMUWA

INDIAN OCEAN

SOUTHERN

Galle ●

Above: Fishermen unload their catch at the end of a day's hard work.

Adam's Peak B4

Bay of Bengal
  B1–D4

Central Province
  B3–C4
Colombo A4

Eastern Province
  C2–D5

Galle B5
Gulf of Mannar
  A2–A3

Indian Ocean
  A5–D5

Kala Oya A2–B3
Kandy B4
Kelani Oya A4–B4
Kirigalpotta B4
Kumbukkan Oya
  C4–D5

Mahaweli Ganga
  C3–C4

North Central
  Province
  B2–C3
North Western
  Province A2–B4
Northern Province
  A1–C2
Nuwara Eliya B4

Palk Bay A1
Palk Strait A1–B1
Pidurutalagala B4
Polonnaruwa C3

Sabaragamuwa
  Province B4–C5
Southern
  Province B5–D5

Uva Province
  C3–C5

Western Province
  A4–B5

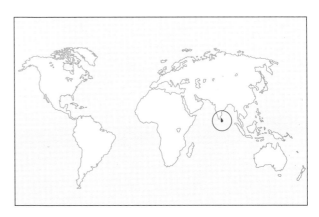

Quick Facts

Official Name	Democratic Socialist Republic of Sri Lanka
Capital	Colombo
Official Languages	Sinhala and Tamil
Population	19,576,783 (July 2002 estimate)
Land Area	25,332 square miles (65,610 square km)
Provinces	Central, Eastern, North Central, North Western, Northern, Sabaragamuwa, Southern, Uva, Western
Highest Point	Pidurutalagala (8,281 feet/2,524 m)
Major Mountains	Adam's Peak, Kirigalpotta
Major Rivers	Mahaweli Ganga, Kala Oya, Kelani Oya, Kumbukkan Oya
Ethnic Groups	Veddahs, Sinhalese, and Tamils
Main Religions	Buddhism, Hinduism, Islam, Christianity
Important Holidays	Sinhalese and Tamil New Year (April 14) Vesak (May), Perahera (July/August) Deepavali (October/November) Christmas (December 25)
Currency	Sri Lankan rupee (97 LKR = U.S. $1 as of 2003)

Opposite: Sri Lanka has many Buddhist statues and temples located all over the island.

Glossary

astrologer: a person who studies the stars and planets and their supposed influence on people's lives.

assassinated: murdered (usually a political leader or prominent person).

baila (BY-lah)**:** an energetic and rhythmic dance in Sri Lanka.

Burghers: descendants of marriages between the Sinhalese and the Dutch or the Sinhalese and the Portuguese.

colonizers: people who settle in or establish a colony.

cricket: a game played with a ball and bat on a large field by two sides of usually eleven players each.

diversified: having a large variety.

embroidery: needlework decorations.

ethnic: relating to a particular race or cultural group.

exorcising: trying to drive out an evil spirit by using a religious or solemn ceremony.

guerilla: a person engaged in warfare as a member of an independent unit.

hoppers (hop-PERS)**:** a pancake-like dish made using rice flour cooked over low heat.

horoscopes: forecasts by astrologers.

kotta pora (koh-TAH POH-rah)**:** a Sri Lankan game featuring pillow fights.

kolam (KOH-lahm)**:** a Sri Lankan dance in which the dancers wear masks.

kovils (KOH-vills)**:** Hindu temples.

lagoons: areas of shallow water that are separated from the ocean by sand dunes.

olinda kaliya (oh-LIN-dah KAH-lee-yah)**:** a board game played using colored seeds.

orphanage: a home for children who have no parents.

parliament: a body of people elected to make and uphold a country's laws.

pension: a fixed amount of money other than wages that is paid to a person on a regular basis in recognition of work done in the past.

pittu (pit-TOOH)**:** a mixture of rice flour and grated coconut steamed in bamboo tubes.

plateaus: areas of high, flat land rising sharply from the surrounding land.

prominent: standing out or attracting attention.

provinces: administrative districts or divisions of a country.

sanctuaries: safe places for wildlife where no hunting is allowed.

snorkeling: swimming underwater with a tube called a snorkel above the surface to provide air.

More Books to Read

Buddha. Hitz Demi (Henry Holt & Co.)

Celebrate in South Asia. Joseph F. Viesti (Lothrop, Lee & Shepard)

Divali. World of Holidays series. Dilip Kadodwala (Raintree/Steck-Vaughn)

A Family in Sri Lanka. Gay Bennett (Lerner)

Hinduism. World Beliefs and Cultures series. Sue Penney (Heinemann)

India and Sri Lanka. Cultures and Costumes series. Conor Kilgallon (Mason Crest)

Prince Siddhartha: The Story of Buddha. Jonathan Landaw (Wisdom Publications)

The Quail's Egg: A Folk Tale from Sri Lanka. Joanna Troughton (Peter Bedrick Books)

Sri Lanka. Cultures of the World series. Nanda Pethiyagoda Wanasundera (Benchmark Books)

Sri Lanka in Pictures. Visual Geography series. (Lerner)

Sri Lanka. Let's Visit series. John C. Caldwell (Burke)

Videos

Elephant. National Geographic Video Classics series. (National Geographic)

Families in the Wild: Monkeys. Just the Facts series. (Goldhil)

Web Sites

lcweb2.loc.gov/frd/cs/lktoc.html

withanage.tripod.com/index.html

www.infoplease.com/ipa/ A0107992.html

www.lankalibrary.com

www.lankachronicle.com/kids.html

www.lanka.net/ctb/

Due to the dynamic nature of the Internet, some web sites stay current longer than others. To find additional web sites, use a reliable search engine with one or more of the following keywords to help you locate information about Sri Lanka. Keywords: *Bandaranaike, Buddhism, Ceylon, Colombo, elephants, Kandy, Sinhalese, Tamils.*

Index